DISCARDED

EXPLORING THE CANADIAN ARCTIC

Northern Industries

by Heather C. Hudak

Weigl

Published by Weigl Educational Publishers Limited
6325 10 Street SE
Calgary, Alberta
T2H 2Z9

www.weigl.com

Library and Archives Canada Cataloguing in Publication

Hudak, Heather C., 1975-
      Northern industries / Heather C. Hudak.

(Exploring the Canadian Arctic)
Includes index.
ISBN 978-1-55388-959-5 (bound).--ISBN 978-1-55388-963-2 (pbk.)

1. Industries--Canada, Northern--Juvenile literature.
I. Title. II. Series: Exploring the Canadian Arctic (Calgary, Alta.)

Printed in the United States of America
1 2 3 4 5 6 7 8 9 0 13 12 11 10 09

Editor: Nick Winnick
Design: Terry Paulhus

Weigl acknowledges Getty Images as its primary image supplier for this title.

We gratefully acknowledge the financial support of the Government of Canada through the Book Publishing Industry Development
Program (BPIDP) for our publishing activities.

Contents

Beyond 60 Degrees

Canada's Arctic region is a vast area that covers more than 40 percent of the country's total land. The Northwest Territories, Yukon, Nunavut, and the northern tip of Quebec make up this northern area.

Any land in Canada above 60 degrees latitude is considered the North. This imaginary line became the border of the Arctic region when Saskatchewan and Alberta were declared provinces in 1905.

Made up of three main biomes—tundra, ocean, and boreal forest—Canada's Arctic has flat lands and mountain zones. There are numerous lakes and rivers, and many islands sit off the coast of the mainland. While often portrayed as a barren land, the Arctic has been rediscovered in recent years. This land is rich in wildlife and natural resources, both of which have led to many industrial opportunities.

Oil is one of the main natural resources found in Canada's North. It is transported to locations throughout North America via pipelines.

Northwest Passage

People have long believed that the Arctic held potential for industry and development. In the 1400s, explorers began embarking on quests to find the elusive Northwest Passage. This northern waterway connects the Atlantic and Pacific Oceans. Originally, it was believed that the Northwest Passage would provide a shorter trade route between Asia and Europe, allowing goods to be transported faster. Though it is believed now that the Inuit and other First Nations actually discovered the Northwest Passage, many European nations funded expeditions to find this route.

In 1497, Italian explorer John Cabot was the first to journey in search of a sea route through present-day North America. Sailing on behalf of England, he reached what is now Newfoundland. Soon, other explorers made similar failed attempts. However, they charted much of Arctic Canada during their efforts. Nearly 80 years after Cabot's first voyage, Sir Martin Frobisher journeyed to North America on behalf on England in search of a northern passage. He reached present-day Frobisher Bay and believed it to be a route to the Pacific Ocean.

In the 1600s and 1700s, explorers continued to search for the Northwest Passage unsuccessfully. In 1845, a failed attempt by Sir John Franklin led Robert McClure to find the famed Northwest Passage. When Franklin's entire crew disappeared on the expedition, explorers were sent to search for the crew. During such an expedition, McClure's team travelled through the Northwest Passage from the Pacific Ocean side. However, their ship became trapped in ice. When they were rescued, McClure and his crew were taken the remaining length of the passage by sledge.

John Franklin has been credited with laying the groundwork for the discovery of the Northwest Passage.

With the discovery of the Northwest Passage came the need to protect it. The Canadian Coast Guard regularly patrols the passage and its surrounding waters.

Roald Amundsen became the first European to travel the waterway successfully in one ship. From 1903 to 1906, Amundsen and a small crew travelled from the Atlantic to the Pacific, spending two winters researching the North Pole before completing the journey.

Though the passage takes about two weeks less time to travel than the more popular route through the Panama Canal, the waterway is frozen most of the year. However, **global warming** is melting the ice in this region. Each year, an area about the size of Lake Superior melts away. In fact, ice in Canada's Arctic has decreased by about 32 percent since the 1960s. As a result, ships can more easily navigate the waterway.

ARCTIC SOVEREIGNTY

While the Arctic and its potential resources have long been of international interest, the area has received more attention in recent years. Much of this is a result of global warming. As ice in the Northwest Passage melts and the shipping route widens, the commercial opportunities of the Arctic's untapped natural resources, such as minerals, fish, and oil, are becoming more apparent. Although Canada believes it should have **sovereignty** over the Northwest Passage, the United States and European Union have long disputed this claim. They believe international law should determine ownership of the waterway, and that multiple nations should come together to govern the area.

Arctic Resources

C anada's Arctic is home to many natural resources, including gas, oil, diamonds, and other minerals. All of these resources are being used to develop industry in the Arctic. This map shows the distribution of these resources throughout the region.

Beaufort Sea

U.S.A.

NORTHWEST
TERRITORIES

YUKON

BRITISH
COLUMBIA

ALBERTA

LEGEND

	oil and gas
	diamond
	gold
	silver
	emerald
	sapphire
	nickel

Arctic Ocean

GREENLAND

Baffin Bay

Davis Strait

NUNAVUT

ASKATCHEWAN

MANITOBA

Hudson Bay

QUEBEC

Mining for Minerals

The Canadian Arctic has a wealth of mineral resources. However, until recently, they were not actively mined. This is because the harsh conditions of the northern environment make it a challenge for people to live and work in the region. Roads and other transportation routes, such as airports, are limited in the North, making it difficult to export the resources to other parts of the country.

Early Aboriginal Peoples used some metals, such as copper, to make tools. However, interest in northern minerals grew when gold was discovered in the Yukon in the late 1800s. During what became known as the Klondike Gold Rush, thousands of people flocked to the Canadian North in search of riches. The events of this gold rush sparked further mineral exploration in the region, and mining continues to be a major industry in the Yukon. Silver, lead, zinc, and copper are other important minerals found in the Yukon.

While mining in Nunavut is a fairly recent pursuit, lead-zinc mines operated in the territory from the 1970s to 2002. Prior to 1962, a nickel mine operated in Rankin Inlet. The Jericho diamond mine opened in 2006. There also is a possibility of gold mining in the area.

Commercial mining began in the Northwest Territories in the 1930s in Port Radium. Later, the government helped fund the establishment of the Pine Point and the Catung mines.

First-hand Account

Robert Service

Robert Service was known as the "Bard of the Yukon" for writing poems about the Canadian North. Service arrived in the Yukon years after the gold rush and worked in a bank.

I wanted the gold, and I sought it;
I scrabbled and mucked like a slave.
Was it famine or scurvy, I fought it;
I hurled my youth into a grave.
I wanted the gold, and I got it --
Came out with a fortune last fall, --
Yet somehow life's not what I thought it,
And somehow the gold isn't all.

From Robert Service's
"The Spell of the Yukon"

Gold and uranium mines were present in the Northwest Territories in the 1950s and 1960s, with the most significant commercial deposits found near Yellowknife and at the Lupin gold mine northwest of Yellowknife. However, when diamonds were discovered in the area in the early 1990s, mining became a booming business venture in the Northwest Territories.

In order to mine the Canadian North, governments, companies, and individuals must comply with certain rules and regulations. To begin, mining must be done in a way that least impacts the environment, wildlife, and people who live in the area. Natural areas that have been identified as key to animals and plants must not be mined, and Aboriginal rights as outlined in treaties, **land claims**, and the Constitution must be respected.

■ The Polaris lead and zinc mine operated on Little Cornwallis Island, in the Northwest Territories, until 2002. At that time, it was the most northerly mine in the world.

THE WORLD'S OLDEST ROCKS

Dating back about four billion years, the world's oldest rocks have been found in northern Quebec. The rocks, which are located along the coast of the Hudson Bay in the Nuvvuagittuq belt, formed about 300 million years after Earth came into existence. Information about Earth's early atmosphere can be gained from studying the rocks. Prior to the discovery of these rocks in 2001, the Acasta Gneiss in the Northwest Territories was the oldest-known outcropping of rocks.

Northern Land Claims

Aboriginal Peoples are Canada's original inhabitants, but with the arrival of European settlers, their claim to the land was threatened. As land was developed for industry, hunting grounds were lost. This had a major impact on the Aboriginal Peoples of the North. Some of the traditions the Inuit and their ancestors had practised were giving way to the ways of life of the European settlers.

Canada's northern Aboriginal Peoples accept the need to develop parts of their traditional lands, but they want to have a voice in the process and a share of profits that may be earned. Providing Aboriginal Peoples with a certain amount of control over northern development has been done largely through land claims.

In the 1970s, northern Aboriginal Peoples were faced with the construction of a natural gas pipeline that would open up their lands to further development. Through public hearings, Aboriginal leaders were able to postpone construction until they could reach land claim agreements with the government.

◼ The Inuit celebrated the creation of Nunavut with the raising of the territorial flag.

The first claim, the Inuvialuit Final Agreement, was reached in 1984. This was followed by the Dene and Métis claims in 1987. The Yukon claim was settled in principle in 1993. Other claims were negotiated separately or are still in negotiation.

The Inuit decided to combine their land claims to negotiate the creation of a new territory. In 1999, the Canadian government divided the Northwest Territories to establish a territory called Nunavut. Covering 351,000 square kilometres of the land, this new territory was given to the Inuit, along with fishing and mining rights for part of the land, and $1.17 billion to help develop the territory.

■ The Nunavut legislative building is located in the territory's capital city, Iqaluit. It is here that many of the decisions relating to the territory and its people are made.

CHECK THIS OUT

Read more about the people and history behind the creation of Nunavut at www.tradition-orale.ca/english/changing-the-face-canada-b33.html.

Digging for Diamonds

In Canada, the quest for diamonds succeeded when a major deposit of these valuable "rocks" was discovered at Point Lake in the Northwest Territories, about 300 kilometres from the capital city of Yellowknife. By 1998, the first diamond mine, Ekati, had opened in the area. Five years later, a second mine, Diavik, opened for business about 100 kilometres southeast of Ekati.

In the first four years of diamond production in Canada, about 13.8 million carats, worth $2.8 billion, were mined. By 2003, Canada was considered a top producer on the world market, ranking third for diamond production after Botswana and Russia.

■ The Diavik diamond mine has its own processing plant, where diamonds are broken from the rock in which they are embedded and sorted.

First-hand Account

Jimmy Larkin

Diamond mining has created new opportunities for people living in the North. Jimmy Larkin, an Aboriginal person residing in Yellowknife, has said that he is grateful for the industry and its impact on his community. Larkin works at Diavik as a heavy-equipment operator.

"If you see something you like go and pursue it. Keep pursuing the goal you set and you will accomplish it... anyone can do it if they set their mind to it."

Since then, two more diamond mines have opened in Canada's North. Jericho, Nunavut's first diamond mine, began production in 2006. Two years later, Snap Lake-4 began operations in the Northwest Territories.

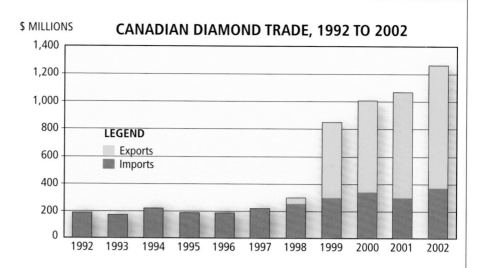

CANADIAN DIAMOND TRADE, 1992 TO 2002

$ MILLIONS

LEGEND
Exports
Imports

Heavy equipment, such as haulers and excavators, are used when mining for diamonds.

Northern Oil and Gas

People had known that the Arctic held oil resources for many years. Long before Europeans arrived in the area, Aboriginal Peoples had used **hydrocarbons** to seal their canoes. When the Europeans arrived, the Aboriginal Peoples showed them locations where oil had seeped to the surface. However, it was not until the early twentieth century—when the usefulness of oil became apparent—that the search for Arctic oil began in earnest.

One of the first important oil finds in the Arctic occurred in 1920 at Norman Wells, on the MacKenzie River in the Northwest Territories. The flow of oil was so strong that the equipment at that time could not contain it. Even with this success, however, oil companies did not rush to the Arctic, mainly due to cost. Many felt that importing oil from other countries would be less expensive than developing oilfields in the Arctic. Still, some oil companies did start staking claims on the land for future use, and a small **refinery** was built at Norman Wells.

First-hand Account

Rond Lake

In 1889, R.G. McConnell of the Geological Survey suggested that Rond Lake, near Fort Good Hope, was a good source of tar.

"The Devonian rocks are nearly everywhere more or less **petroliferous** and over large areas afford promising indications of the presence of oil in workable quantities...The possible oil country along the Mackenzie valley is thus seen to be almost co-extensive with that of the valley itself. Its remoteness from the present centres of population and its situation north of the still un-worked Athabasca and Peace River oil field will probably delay its development for some years to come, but this is only a question of time."

■ Pipelines were being built as early as the 1940s to carry oil from locations such as Norman Wells to Whitehorse.

During World War II, both Canada and the United States realized that it was necessary to secure their continental oil resources. As a result, Arctic oilfield development increased. A pipeline was constructed that ran from Norman Wells to a refinery in Whitehorse. From there, it was sent to Alaska via another pipeline. Drilling increased at Norman Wells as well, with the addition of 60 more wells.

■ Oil drilling ships are currently searching for oil in the Beaufort Sea. They remain on the pack ice through the winter months.

Following the war, oil and gas companies continued their exploration of the Arctic, moving farther and farther north, eventually reaching the islands north of the mainland. A well was drilled at Drake Point on Melville Island in 1969, and a significant gas discovery was made. This encouraged even more exploration and development of the area, with more exciting finds made.

In 1977, however, the Canadian government asked for a 10-year **moratorium** on the construction of a major pipeline in order to have time to settle land claims with the area's Aboriginal Peoples. This did not stop companies from developing the area's oil resources, but it did slow their progress. Today, with many land claims now settled, oil and gas companies are increasing their activity in the Arctic.

MCKENZIE VALLEY GAS PROJECT

In an effort to supply northern gas across North America, a pipeline has been proposed along the Mackenzie Valley in the Northwest Territories. The 1,220-kilometre-long natural gas pipeline will connect onshore gas fields in the North with markets located to the south. The project aims to be transporting gas through the pipeline in 2010 and will include natural gas fields in Parsons Lake, Taglu, and Niglintgak, as well as a gas processing facility in the Inuvik area. Natural gas pipelines will run from the Inuvik area to northwestern Alberta and Norman Wells.

Co-operative Business

Traditional art and crafts is a major industry in the Canadian Arctic. People around the world collect art, such as wall hangings, prints, carvings, and jewellery.

When people of European ancestry began settling in the North, northern peoples wanted to preserve some of their traditions. In the 1950s and 1960s, they began forming community-owned **co-operatives** to sell traditional goods and services, such as art, furs, and seafood. Over time, these co-operatives grew to include businesses such as retail stores, hotels, and post offices.

Soon, the Canadian government stepped in to help improve the Arctic economy. As a result of the government's efforts, Canadian Arctic Producers was created to sell arts and crafts made by northern peoples. This group buys products from artists and makes them available to stores and collectors all over the world. Interest in traditional art quickly grew, surpassing fur sales as the area's main industry. In the early 1970s, the Canadian Arctic Co-operatives Federation formed to provide management services to co-operative members and help them grow their businesses.

Today, many artists belong to Arctic Co-operatives Limited. This group markets their work and obtains the best price. Co-operative members buy shares in the company, so they are also owners of the group. Each member has equal say in the affairs of the co-operative.

MARK TOTAN
INUK ARTIST

Hailing from Igloolik, Nunavut, Mark Totan is a self-taught soapstone artist. Using a hammer, chisel, and hand ax, Mark carves figures from stone blocks, showing the history, symbols, and traditional ways of Aboriginal Peoples. Mark began carving in 1988, learning the trade from an older master carver. His work can be found in galleries across Canada, parts of the United States, and in private collections around the world. His sons, Tony and Clivelon, are carvers as well.

As a symbol of the Arctic, the polar bear is a common subject in Inuit sculpture.

Printmakers require special skills and equipment to make prints suitable for the international market.

Some art galleries in Canada specialize in Inuit art.

Traditionally, the Inuit used masks when dancing to express their spiritual beliefs.

Inuit prints are often created with the help of stencils.

A Way of Life

Hunting and fishing have always been important to northern people. In fact, hunting and fishing supplies about 40 percent of the food Aboriginal Peoples eat in the North. Many of the techniques used in the past to hunt and fish, and prepare the food for eating are still used today. Over time, hunting and fishing have shifted from being necessities of survival to commercial industries.

THEN	NOW
THE NEED FOR SURVIVAL	
Inuit families or communities would hunt and fish only as much as they needed for survival. Traditionally, hunting and fishing were done as a way to supply northern peoples with food, clothing, and shelter.	In Nunavut, commercial fishing earns about $14 million each year. Turbot, shrimp, and Arctic char are the main catches. Most fish are sold at stores across Canada and the United States. In the Yukon, trapping animals such as muskrat and lynx supplies some of the pelts for Canada's fur industry.
SEAL HUNTING	
Seal hunting was a way of life for northern Aboriginal Peoples. The meat was used to feed their families, and the pelts were used for clothing. Furs were also sold on the world market.	Seal hunting is still done for food, but the demand for seal fur has decreased dramatically in recent years.
FISHING METHODS	
In summer, Inuit fished from kayaks. During winter, they would make holes in the ice to catch fish. Three-pronged spears, nets, and fishing lines were common tools.	Traditional fishing methods are still used by many Inuit to supply food for their family or community. However, some companies use modern equipment, such as trawlers, to fish on a larger scale.
HUNTING METHODS	
When hunting game, the Inuit used spears, bows and arrows, and clubs. They used a special knife called an ulu to skin animals and prepare the meat. They used dogsleds to travel to hunting sites.	Traditional hunting methods are still used, but snowmobiles are used for hunting more often than dogsleds.
FOOD STORAGE	
Most times, fresh meat was eaten raw. Sometimes, it was frozen or dried and preserved for later use.	Meat can be stored in a freezer, but it is also dried on outdoor meat racks. Other foods, such as fruit and vegetables and canned goods, can be purchased in stores. However, foods cost about 30 percent more to purchase in places such as Nunavut because of high transportation costs.

Seal
Hunting

AT ISSUE

Seal hunting is a traditional way of life for the Inuit. For thousands of years, they have used these animals for food, shelter, oil, and clothing. No part of the seal is wasted.

Over time, however, seal hunting has become a commercial activity. Many Inuit now earn an income from this activity. Each year, hundreds of thousands of seals are killed for their fur. There is a limited market for their meat, so most of the seal is unused. Still, in 2004 and 2005, sealing earned about $16.5 million in product sales.

The Royal Commission on Seals and Sealing in Canada has said that clubbing and shooting are the most humane ways known to kill seals. However, this has sparked much debate. Often, these hunting methods are not done properly, resulting in a painful death for the animal. While animal rights groups are not opposed to traditional Inuit hunting, they have demanded better regulations for commercial sealing.

In May 2009, the European Union (EU) announced that it would no longer accept commercial seal hunt products. As the EU is the main customer for Canada's seal products, the result is a huge loss to the industry's annual earnings.

Should Commercial Sealing Be Allowed?

A debate occurs when people research opposing viewpoints on an issue and argue them following a special format and rules. Debating is a useful skill that helps people express their opinions on specific subjects.

1. Decide how you feel about the issue described.
2. Ask a friend to argue the opposing viewpoint.
3. Use the information in this book and other sources to prepare a two-minute statement about your viewpoint.
4. Present your argument, and listen while a friend gives his or her argument. Make notes, and prepare a response.
5. Present your rebuttal and a final statement. Let your friend do the same. Did your friend's arguments change how you feel about the issue?

Tourism

Tourism is a growing industry in Canada's Arctic, with people coming from all parts of the world to experience the vibrant northern setting. During their visit, they are able to experience the unique culture, wildlife, and nature of the region.

CRUISING

Cruise ships offer many routes through Arctic waterways. While touring on board these water-bound vessels, passengers may have views of ice floes and fjords, as well as wildlife, such as polar bears and whales. On land, they can visit remote villages to experience the way of life of Canada's northern communities.

ARTS AND CULTURE

Visits to northern communities provide insight into the way people live and work in this unique environment. By spending time in these communities, tourists are introduced to the food, clothing, artwork, music, dance, and languages of the various Aboriginal groups that make up Arctic Canada.

WILDLIFE VIEWING

Polar bears, walruses, beluga and white whales, narwhals, moose, wood bison, and caribou are just some of the animals that are found in the Arctic. Guides and boats can be hired to take tourists on excursions to witness these creatures in their natural habitats. There also are many bird sanctuaries throughout the region.

As more people choose the Arctic as their vacation destination, the industry grows and is able to provide tourists with the opportunity to have different kinds of experiences. These are just a few examples of tourist activities found in Arctic Canada.

CANOEING AND KAYAKING

The numerous rivers carved throughout the Arctic provide scenic canoe routes. Often, these routes cross through protected areas that are home to many endangered plants and animals. Kayaking along the coast is a popular tourist activity in the North.

CAMPING AND HIKING

There are many scenic places to hike, or pitch a tent and camp in the Arctic. From wildlife reserves to national parks, the varied landscapes provide a natural adventure. In some places, the northern lights encircle the night sky.

FISHING AND HUNTING

Fishing is a common activity in the North. In many places, fishing sites are accessible only by bushplane, and tourists are welcome to stay at luxury lodges. Many tourists also come to the area to participate in sport hunting. Muskox, walrus, caribou, polar bear, and wolves are among the animals tourists hunt in the North.

Northern Parks

Canada is known for its vast natural areas that seem to stretch endlessly across the nation. In an effort to preserve natural areas of special significance, the Canadian government has established a system of national parks that can be found in every one of Canada's ten provinces and three territories. Ranging in size from 9 square kilometres to 45,000 square kilometres, these natural areas showcase Canada's diverse plant and animal life. People travel from all over the world to visit these impressive parks, taking part in outdoor activities, such as camping, hiking, and kayaking, as they tour the breathtaking landscape.

AULAVIK NATIONAL PARK OF CANADA
Area: 12,000 square kilometres
Special features:
- name means "place where people travel"
- home to the world's highest density of muskoxen, as well as the endangered Peary caribou
- has been inhabited by people for nearly 4,000 years

AUYUITTUQ NATIONAL PARK OF CANADA
Area: 19,089 square kilometres
Special features:
- named for the Inuktitut word meaning "land that never melts"
- plantlife covers only 15 percent of the area
- created in 1976

IVVAVIK NATIONAL PARK OF CANADA
Area: 10,168 square kilometres
Special features:
- was the first national park established as a result of a land claim agreement between the Inuvialuit of the Western Arctic and the Government of Canada
- home to the British Mountains, which cover about two-thirds of the park
- contain the calving grounds for the porcupine caribou herd

KLUANE NATIONAL PARK AND RESERVE OF CANADA
Area: 21,980 square kilometres
Special features:
- made a **World Heritage Site** in 1979
- has the largest non-polar ice fields in the world
- home to Mount Logan, Canada's highest mountain

NAHANNI NATIONAL PARK RESERVE OF CANADA
Area: 4765.2 square kilometres
Special features:
- declared a World Heritage Site in 1978
- has the richest diversity of plantlife of any area similar in size in the continental Northwest Territories
- has a visitor centre at Fort Simpson

QUTTINIRPAAQ NATIONAL PARK OF CANADA
Area: 37,775 square kilometres
Special features:
- has continuous daylight in the summer
- much of it is an Arctic desert
- has rocks that formed more than one billion years ago

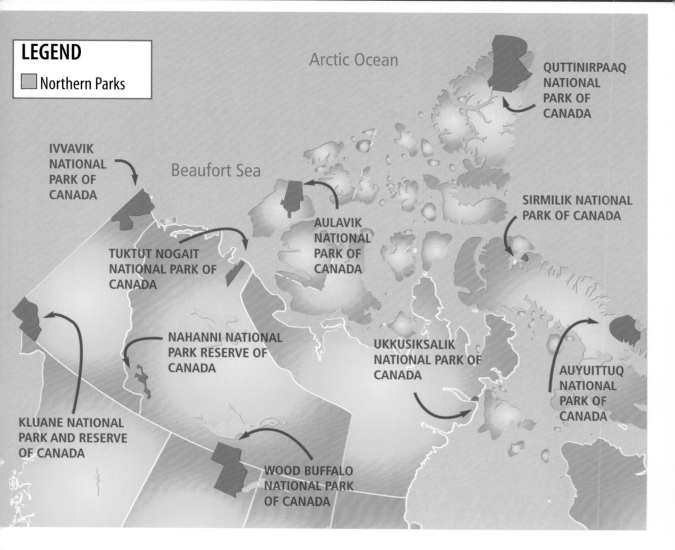

Arctic Ocean

Beaufort Sea

QUTTINIRPAAQ NATIONAL PARK OF CANADA

IVVAVIK NATIONAL PARK OF CANADA

SIRMILIK NATIONAL PARK OF CANADA

AULAVIK NATIONAL PARK OF CANADA

TUKTUT NOGAIT NATIONAL PARK OF CANADA

NAHANNI NATIONAL PARK RESERVE OF CANADA

UKKUSIKSALIK NATIONAL PARK OF CANADA

AUYUITTUQ NATIONAL PARK OF CANADA

KLUANE NATIONAL PARK AND RESERVE OF CANADA

WOOD BUFFALO NATIONAL PARK OF CANADA

SIRMILIK NATIONAL PARK OF CANADA
Area: 22,252 square kilometres
Special features:
- made up of three areas—Bylot Island, Oliver Sound, and Borden Peninsula
- named after the Inuktitut word meaning "the place of the glaciers"
- established in 2001

TUKTUT NOGAIT NATIONAL PARK OF CANADA
Area: 28,190 square kilometres
Special features:
- created to protect the breeding grounds of the bluenose herd of barren-ground caribou
- has more than 360 archaeological sites
- has an average temperature of −11 degrees Celsius

UKKUSIKSALIK NATIONAL PARK OF CANADA
Area: 20,500 square kilometres
Special features:
- has more than 500 archaeological sites
- is Canada's 41st national park
- was the location of a Hudson's Bay Company trading post from 1925 to 1947

WOOD BUFFALO NATIONAL PARK OF CANADA
Area: 44,807 square kilometres
Special features:
- Canada's largest national park
- created in 1922 to protect free-roaming bison
- became a World Heritage Site in 1983

Quiz

What have you learned about the industries of the Canadian Arctic? Take this quiz to find out.

1 When did the Klondike's Gold Rush occur?

2 Name four minerals found in Canada's Arctic.

3 What are the names of the first two diamond mines in Canada's North?

4 How have the Aboriginal Peoples of Canada's Arctic been able to secure control over northern development?

5 Where was the Arctic's first important oilfield found?

6 How is oil transferred from the Arctic to other parts of the country?

7 What types of businesses have been formed to sell the arts and crafts of northern peoples?

8 Why do the Inuit traditionally hunt seals?

9 How much money does commercial fishing bring in to Nunavut each year?

10 Name six tourism activities in the North.

Answers:
1. Late 1800s
2. Gold, diamond, lead, zinc, nickel, uranium, silver, copper
3. Ekati and Diavik
4. Land claims
5. Norman Wells
6. Pipelines
7. Co-operatives
8. For food, clothing, shelter, and oil
9. Approximately $14 million
10. Cruising, hunting, fishing, arts and culture, wildlife viewing, canoeing, kayaking, camping, and hiking

Mining Safety

Mining can be dangerous. As tunnels are made deeper in the ground, there is greater pressure on the walls. This can cause the tunnel to cave in. Mine designers look for ways to keep this from happening. Try this experiment to see if you can build a safe mine.

What you will need
Sand
Measuring cup
Tape
Sheets of paper
Water
Scissors
One small cardboard box
One large cardboard box

1. Cut a 5-centimetre hole on the front and back sides of the small box.

2. Open the larger box, and place the small box inside.

3. Use paper and tape to make a tube that will act as a tunnel.

4. Slide the paper tunnel through the holes in the small box. It should hang out about 2.5 centimetres long on each side of the box.

5. Pour a small amount of water on the sand, and mix together using your hands.

6. Use the measuring cup to fill the small box with sand, covering the tunnel until it caves in. You will need to look through the holes in the box to see when the paper flattens. Be sure to keep track of how much sand you used.

7. Make more tunnels using different designs, and try step 6 again. Does it take more or less sand to make the tunnel cave in? Which design was stronger?

Further Research

Many books and websites provide information on the industries of Canada's Arctic. To learn more about these industries, borrow books from the library, or surf the Internet.

Most libraries have computers that connect to a database for researching information. If you input a key word, you will be provided with a list of books in the library that contain information on that topic. Nonfiction books are arranged numerically, using their call number. Fiction books are organized alphabetically by the author's last name.

Books

Beehag, Graham. *Fishing* (Canadian Industries series). Calgary, Alberta: Weigl Educational Publishers Limited, 2007.

Matthews, Sheelagh. *Mining* (Canadian Industries series). Calgary, Alberta: Weigl Educational Publishers Limited, 2007.

Tomljanovic, Tatiana. *Energy* (Linking Canadian Communities series). Calgary, Alberta: Weigl Educational Publishers Limited, 2008.

Websites

To find out more about Canada's claim to the Arctic, visit **www.thecanadianencyclopedia.com**, and enter "Arctic sovereignty" into the search engine.

Read about the Diavik diamond mine at **www.diavik.ca**.

For information about the Arctic, check out **http://polar.nrcan.gc.ca/arctic/index_e.php**.

Glossary

co-operatives: business organizations owned and operated by a group of people for their mutual benefit

global warming: a sustained increase in the average temperature of the Earth's atmosphere

hydrocarbons: organic compounds which contain only carbon and hydrogen; fossil fuels, such as oil, are made up of hydrocarbons

land claims: legal declarations of desired control over areas of property

moratorium: a period during which certain proceedings or obligations are suspended

petroliferous: a rock containing oil

refinery: an industrial plant that converts crude oil into usable fuel products

sovereignty: the exclusive right to control a government, a country, a people, or oneself

World Heritage Site: a place designated by the United Nations to have cultural signficance on a global level

Index